# London Memories

## IAN WHITMARSH and KEVIN ROBERTSON

Ian Allan
PUBLISHING

# Introduction

Both as a tourist destination as well as a centre for global commerce, London ranks high in the league of world cities. The business side of the city we may not dwell upon for the present, as this is an album of nostalgia intended to rekindle lost memories as well as hopefully encouraging others to seek out the well-known and more secret locations of this great city.

The inspiration for the book came from an unsolicited e-mail in 2005. Would I be interested in viewing a selection of colour material, road and rail, from the collection of the late Ian Whitmarsh? Such an invitation could not be resisted, and it was not long before I was being both entertained and regaled with box upon box of quality material depicting London road and rail covering a 25-year period from the mid-1960s onwards.

The slides had been taken by Ian Tarrant Whitmarsh, and which, following his untimely death, had fortunately survived in the hands of his family. Ian was born on 18 May 1948 and would later recount one of his earliest memories as walking by the River Thames with his mother, his younger sister in a pram.

Living ninety-two stairs up in a third-floor flat above Westminster Bank, it was a treat to be taken out for a ride on the back of his father's bicycle after work on a summer's evening. In 1951 the family moved to Southall, Middlesex, where Whitmarsh would develop an interest and lifetime obsession in chasing steam trains. He also joined the many trainspotters regularly to be seen on the footbridge spanning the Great Western line by Southall station.

An early essay praised at school described his travels discovering London. Whether visiting museums, the sights or an exhibition at Earls Court or Olympia, they were accessible using the buses, trains or Underground. A No 65 from Ealing Broadway would take you all the way to Chessington Zoo. A London Transport Red Rover ticket for the day would cover travel on red buses, starting on the 207 that would stop outside his front door. Routemaster buses replaced the old 607 trolleybuses, which ran from Shepherd's Bush Green all along the Uxbridge Road through Acton, Ealing, Hanwell, Southall, Hayes and Hillingdon turning round at Uxbridge. A Green Rover ticket would take him further afield on the country buses starting from Uxbridge. Ian's extensive knowledge of the route numbers and their destinations caused an aunt to liken him to a talking timetable!

A Sunday morning family trip to pay a visit to a grandfather in Walworth would often include a stopover to East Street market. Alternatively, a stop on the way through London might be to see The Changing of the Guard or a walk along The Embankment towards Tower Bridge. After attending Southall Grammar school, Whitmarsh's first job was at Brentford Market for

---

*Front cover:* A moment in time. Against a backdrop of contemporary advertising the 1956 generation is captured for posterity. (Note especially the British Road Services lorry and railway container attempting to fight its way into the — even then — endless stream of traffic.) *Author's collection*

*Back cover:* A reminder of past days, a horse bus but now in use as a tourist attraction outside Baker Street station on 15 September 1979. Next stop No 221b...? *Ian Whitmarsh*

*Previous page:* What is in some respect is almost a silhouette of parts of Trafalgar Square seeming devoid of visitors. Visible are the two fountains and the façade of the National Gallery behind. According to the Mayor of London, since the Square was pedestrianised in 2002, visitor numbers to the area have increased by 200% and there are also now wardens to assist and direct the public. *Author's collection*

First published 2007
Reprinted 2007

ISBN (10) 0 7110 3232 7
ISBN (13) 978 0 7110 3232 3

Published by Ian Allan Publishing

an imprint of Ian Allan Publishing Ltd, Hersham, Surrey KT12 4RG
Printed in England by Ian Allan Printing Ltd, Hersham, Surrey KT12 4RG

Code: 0712/A

Visit the Ian Allan Publishing website at www.ianallanpublishing.com

Geo Munro & Sons. He would later work in Covent Garden and finally for an international logistics company. Photographing images of London and transport took over at an early age when he began to document the names and numbers of buses and trains. His early works were shot on black and white film but he soon adopted the use of colour. Trips were made all over the country and his slide collection recorded working images of the last trams of Blackpool, regional bus companies and Britain's final steam trains. As steam transport disappeared from Britain, Whitmarsh and a group of enthusiasts visited China and South America where the use of steam continued. In all, Whitmarsh had recorded some 35,000 individual frames.

However, an album that consisted of trains and buses may not necessarily be to everyone's taste — especially when the writer may not possess the unique knowledge of the photographer, nor his insight into the conditions of the time. Accordingly, and after discussion with the publisher, it was decided to broaden the net and include photographic views of London from other collections. Therefore, I am grateful to all those who have placed their precious material at

Road travel between cities, 1950s style. This is the London to Liverpool express coach service posed with other vehicles outside a regular stop at the Whitbread 'Harrow', Studley Green and before the era of the motorway service area. *Author's collection*

my disposal. The individual photographers have been credited accordingly. Gentlemen, I thank you all.

London is a charismatic city whose nightlife is famous — as the sun goes down, neon signs and lights illuminate the capital. Indeed, aside from the dark days of war, the lights of London blaze as a beacon for all to recognise: a symbol of freedom and expression. The city and its environment are ever changing, be it through building development or fashion — the latter covering not just clothing but the requirements and expectations of Londoners themselves. And more recently, London has seen a shift of focus towards environmental issues, which has meant that transport has had to adapt to being 'green'.

Further change is promised in the coming years as well; changes that Whitmarsh could not have foreseen but would no doubt have approved. Improved transport links to the proposed new Olympic Village and the Heathrow Express: just two examples of how transport is changing — literally never standing still. However, it is regrettable to learn, in the opinion of the author, that retrograde steps are in process — the fast Gatwick Express train service is currently under threat. For the public to use public transport, it must be seen to be both attractive, and if the opportunity presents itself, forward moving. Travelling backwards should not be an option.

Additionally, in so far as transport is concerned, the Routemaster buses are no more, steam trains have disappeared and there has been a renaissance in the waterways, both in their use and also in their condition and cleanliness. London has always been a cosmopolitan city, individuals from differing races, creeds and backgrounds mixing amongst one another as well as maintaining their own individual preferred areas, mostly without threat or fear to the pre-existing community. It may safely be said that London has expanded to form a metropolis bounded in recent years by the M25. And quite possibly, if the talk of a second outer-orbital comes to fruition, then the boundaries may be pushed further still.

With possibly just one exception, the theme for this book has also been to keep within the present-day motorway boundary. The exception is the solitary view of the London to Liverpool coach service near Stokenchurch. The quality of this alone makes its inclusion worthwhile, and besides, London was the starting point!

It has been a privilege to be asked to take this opportunity to write *London Memories* and I am also grateful to Ian Whitmarsh whom I never met but sincerely wish I had. I would also like to thank Molly, Janet and Peter for allowing me free rein of the collection.

*Kevin Robertson*

How does anyone commence a photographic tour of London? A location typical to London has to be the answer, but if so which one? Possibly the best known of all London landmarks is Big Ben on the corner of the Houses of Parliament and seen here from Parliament Square. In truth, the popular name Big Ben does not refer to the clock tower but to the thirteenth bell within. Curiously, the bell also uses old pennies (£/s/d) as counterweights. This was the scene on a summer's day in 1964; even 40 years ago traffic was heavy. As with so many views in this collection, it is not just the buildings themselves but the vehicles, fashions and advertisements that give that certain nostalgia feeling. *Chris Webb*

*Above:* Ludgate Circus in the heart of what is now EC4 and with the unmistakable view of St Paul's Cathedral in the background. It was near here that the Great Fire of 1666 commenced, to be followed two centuries later in 1858 by what was referred to as the 'Great Stink'. Both events are well documented in the history books of the city, and although tragic at the time, were a turning point in social reform. This view was taken during 1963. *Chris Webb*

*Above:* A high vantage point looking down on Eastbourne Terrace alongside Paddington station in late 1962. On the extreme left is the cab road for the station whilst the crossroads has Praed Street to the left and Craven Road on the right. Ahead is West Street. The image seemingly indicates absolute chaos at the junction although it must be remembered that this was just a brief moment in time. *Chris Webb*

*Above:* Another unmistakable sight, Tower Bridge, seen from the north side of the river. Appropriately named after the Tower of London, its foundations were commenced in April 1886 and the bridge was eventually completed eight years later at a cost of £3 million. (Equivalent to £252 million in today's money.) *Chris Webb*

*Right:* Trafalgar Square in 1956 — key to this view has to be the advertising and design of motor vehicles of the day. A popular meeting point, it is possible to book the square for various private/public functions although its most famous role remains playing host to the traditional New Year's Eve party. *Author's collection*

*Above:* The ritual of the Changing of the Guard at Buckingham Palace, a daily 45-minute ceremony. This is another 1956 view, and although there has always been security at royal residences, it was less noticeable during the 1950s. In the background is another famous London feature: the palace balcony where the Royal Family acknowledge the public on special occasions. *Author's collection*

*Right:* Tourists and pigeons enjoying the winter sunshine in Trafalgar Square. On the right is the statue of Sir Henry Havelock, a hero of foreign wars during the 19th century British Empire and whose name also graced numerous roads throughout England. *Author's collection*

A seemingly deserted Westminster Bridge. This is the second structure on the site and dates from 1862, replacing an 1850 masonry bridge that had proved expensive and difficult to maintain. For those with a head for figures, the present structure consists of seven spans varying in length from 94ft to 120ft and supported on piers 10ft wide. The roadway accounts for a width of just over 58ft whilst each pavement is an additional 13ft. *Author's collection*

From the vantage point of the Shell Centre on the South Bank, this 1964 view looks north across the river with Charing Cross station prominent. The railway crosses the river by Hungerford Bridge with pedestrian footpaths alongside. Also visible is part of the Embankment, whilst to the left are various governmental buildings including what were then the Ministry of Agriculture, Fisheries and Food and the Ministry of Defence. *Chris Webb*

( 11 )

*Left:* Battersea Power Station and a classic example of how tastes and favours change over the years. Originally proposed in 1927, the scheme for a power station evoked a storm of protest although its function in generating power for London for over 40 years cannot be denied. The building owes its design to Sir Giles Gilbert Scott who was also responsible for Liverpool Cathedral, Bankside Power Station and Waterloo Bridge as well as the iconic red telephone box. Following its decommissioning as a power station in 1980, the structure was awarded a listed building status although its future has yet to be established. *Author's collection*

*Above left:* Piccadilly Circus and contemporary adverts and styles from the mid-1950s. Here is the intersection between several of the great London thoroughfares: Regent Street, Haymarket, Piccadilly and Shaftesbury Avenue. Traditionally, it has been said that a road snarl-up is as bad as 'Piccadilly Circus'. *Author's collection*

Above right: Moving to the suburbs in May 1964 and a view of St John's Church in Hillingdon, the earliest part of which dates back as far as 1270. Shown here is the famous tower that dates from 1629. Despite its historic origins, this church is still very much a surviving place of worship. *Ian Whitmarsh*

*Far left:* Philip Hardwick's famous Doric Arch at the entrance to Euston station, recorded during its demolition in 1962. Built in 1837/1838 at a cost of £35,000, its demolition created a national outcry — such was the fashion for modern buildings however, historical relics like this were allowed to disappear. There was talk for many years that some of the stonework was retained but this cannot be confirmed. The two gate lodges either side of the arch were retained and stand in Euston Road. *Author's collection*

*Left:* Contemporary with the destruction of the Doric Arch was the Euston Great Hall, although to be more strictly accurate, it was not opened until 1849. Foremost amongst its features were the ceiling and staircase, the building used for many years for an annual carol service. Despite being fully refurbished by its owners, British Railways, in 1953, it was similarly demolished in 1962. *Author's collection*

*Right:* Basking in the shadow of modern post boxes, this Victorian relic was recorded in Sydenham Hill in the summer of 1976. This particular style of post box originated in 1859 and is widely regarded as the first standard design to evolve. Such boxes were eventually replaced due to their letter slots being considered too small to accept larger items. *Ian Whitmarsh*

*Left:* The original Guinness Clock in Battersea Park which was erected in May 1951 in connection with the Festival of Britain. Standing 25 feet high, it was also known as the 'Crazy Clock' and was one of several that Guinness would make featuring animals that were part of their period advertising campaign. Similar but smaller clocks were made for temporary assignments around the UK. By October 1966, spare parts were becoming increasingly difficult to obtain and the company's advertisement campaign was to change. The result was that all clocks were scrapped although one miniature version still survives in the Guinness brewery in Dublin. *Author's collection*

*Right:* Contemporary shop window display recorded in 1962 on a trip to London. This was not a museum but an actual shop surviving at the time although such displays were becoming an increasing rarity with the introduction of the supermarket. *Chris Webb*

*Far left:* The remains of the former Coronet Cinema at 275 High Street, Brentford, the oldest cinema in the borough and in use from 1912 to around 1930. There were two functioning cinemas in the area at the time although the Coronet had been converted to a motor garage by 1934 and the base of a plating company thirty years later. This view was taken in September 1977. *Ian Whitmarsh*

*Left:* Piccadilly Circus recorded on the evening of 5 December 1962 and the day before what was referred to as the 'Great Fog'. The 1962 phenomenon lasted three days and claimed the lives of more than 100 people. Indeed so bad was the weather, not just in London but also over a wide swathe of the country, that it was reported that bus conductors had to walk in front of their vehicles to guide the drivers. *Chris Webb*

*Right:* One can almost sense the eerie sensation associated with the weather that evening. Neon lighting from the advertising hoardings had penetrated the gloom although the unseen build-up of noxious sulphur-dioxide was responsible for many of the fatalities. *Chris Webb*

*Left:* Less troubled times and advertising for the 1962 film *Pressure Point* starring Sidney Poitier, based on the novel by Stanley Kramer. This powerful movie is regarded as groundbreaking even by today's standards. Poitier played the part of a prison psychiatrist tasked with treating a disturbed inmate. *Author's collection*

*Below left:* Christmas 1962 and part of the decorations in Oxford Street that featured stars and angels. Unfortunately nobody considered what would happen if the illuminated angels collected rainwater and they eventually fused. The remedy was to drill drain holes in the bottom part of the angels although this gave the impression that they were relieving themselves on occasion. *Chris Webb*

*Right:* May 1962 and the end of the London trolleybus. This is No 657 and the last service to leave the depot at Isleworth. Environmentally clean, quiet and with a rapid acceleration, it is a shame that the renaissance for tramways in recent years has not been followed with a similar resurgence of the trolleybus. *Chris Webb*

*Above:* Preceding the Routemaster was the RT type of bus, represented here by RT4692 at Hayes End on 27 May 1961. The RT design first entered service in 1939 and there were several variants including those with a wide body, designated RTW. Most were out of service by the mid to late 1960s. *Ian Whitmarsh*

*Right:* RT3213 recorded in the then standard London Country livery of the period. It was photographed at Uxbridge on 27 March 1964. According to one source, driving one of these vehicles took some getting used to as the driver's seat was attached to the bodywork whereas the steering wheel was affixed to the chassis. The result was that on a rough road or if encountering a pothole, the impression was given that body and chassis were about to become detached. *Ian Whitmarsh*

*Left:* A final view of an RT — 2875 is depicted at Northolt station. The radiator blind which was typical on numerous vehicles of the period can be seen. *Ian Whitmarsh*

*Above:* The iconic London Routemaster, seen here in the shape of RM545 at Hayes End on 17 May 1964. Much has been written of these vehicles in their final years, official sources stating they were environmentally unfriendly, costly to operate and a danger to passengers with their open rear platform. The environmental issue may well be true but new or modified engines could have been provided. Operating costs were based on the need for a conductor but what price the peace of mind of the passengers? Surely a flat-fare scheme with passengers purchasing their own tickets would have been the answer. On the grounds of safety, the 'spin' really took off: "There was risk of injury or worse to persons getting on and off a moving bus." Surely this must be put into perspective: how many accidents against how many trips and how many passengers? In 2007 we need protecting from the so-called protectors. *Ian Whitmarsh*

*Left:* This time it is the turn of RM2178, captured on film in Brixton on 18 September 1986 and bound for Crystal Palace. Take a look at the routeing of the second Routemaster which is bound for the same destination and gives some truth to the oft quoted phrase that you wait for ages and then several come along at the same time. *Ian Whitmarsh*

*Above:* Another Brixton view from the same date but included as an example of the flexibility in service allowed by the open platform. Also notice on its side the change from the original London Transport wording to a simpler plain white decal. *Ian Whitmarsh*

*Above:* A final example of Routemaster liveries is this view of SRM20 in the 1977 Silver Jubilee colours for the commemoration of that year. The vehicle was recorded at the junction of Parliament Street and Whitehall and close by the junctions for Richmond Terrace and Downing Street on 29 August 1977. *Ian Whitmarsh*

*Right:* One of several innovative measures in the 1970s and 1980s for London bus transport was the 'Shoplinker' service. The idea was that passengers could board a distinctly coloured vehicle, which was scheduled to take a tour of the renowned shopping areas. All this for a set fare of 30p — LT had already had the idea promoted earlier! Whilst certainly distinctive, the livery was perhaps a bit too garish for the times. RM2159 was photographed at Marble Arch in May 1979. *Tony Molyneaux*

*Above:* Another variation in livery to commemorate 150 years of London Buses since the horse buses of George Shillibeer, whose colours were applied to several vehcles during 1979. RM2142 is seen on the 140 service from Heathrow Airport to Mill Hill on Sunday 11 March 1979. *Tony Molyneaux*

*Right:* Contemporary with the RT was the single-deck RF type; RF319 is seen at Hampton Court station in September 1965. These vehicles were particularly versatile, and as well as appearing in a variety of liveries, were also to be found employed on limited-stop and coach work on occasions. *Ian Whitmarsh*

*Left:* RF567 late in its life and re-liveried with the London Country logo of the period. First entering service back in 1951, the type had a working life of just less than 30 years. Whilst nowadays we take one-man operation for granted, it must be remembered that the early single-deck vehicles also carried a conductor. Photographed in July 1976 at Kingston, according to the destination blind the vehicle is bound for Bookham near Leatherhead. *Ian Whitmarsh*

*Above:* RF571 is seen outside Uxbridge station in May 1964. Despite their diminutive size, these vehicles could accommodate 39 passengers: 38 forward-facing and one sideways behind the driver. A variation in bodywork to create a raised portion for the seating at the rear saw a number of this chassis working for BEA in the 1950s. *Ian Whitmarsh*

*Above:* The new era: M1067, recorded in Clapham Park Road en route for Peckham on 18 September 1986. The vehicle was built by Metro-Cammell-Weymann, hence the MCW insignia, and was one of several hundred of this type introduced in the early 1980s as replacements for the Routemaster. *Ian Whitmarsh*

*Right:* One-man operation was a relatively new concept to Londoners even in 1984; hence this one-year-old front-entrance vehicle has the reminder notice to passengers. Recorded outside the St Boniface Social Club in Tooting 'Mitre', the vehicle is not far from its eventual destination. *Ian Whitmarsh*

*Above:* The intended standard Leyland Atlantean in London Country livery at Harlow in the period 1976/7. Again notice the set fare schedule. In the distance behind is another similar vehicle whilst sandwiched in between at the roadworks is a Ford 'D' series lorry. JPL 180K was allotted fleet number AN80. *Ian Whitmarsh*

*Right:* Variations in livery were not confined to earlier types, as witness the smart colours on this Leyland Fleetline, D2629, painted to celebrate the centenary of Croydon Corporation Tramways. This vehicle was photographed at Chiswick on 2 July 1983. *Tony Molyneaux*

*Left:* Finally in this series of vehicles is a London Buslines example, DM1064, recorded running alongside Brunel's Wharncliffe Viaduct. The livery is also somewhat reminiscent of that used for Bournemouth Corporation vehicles, amongst others, for many years. *Ian Whitmarsh*

*Above:* The Leyland National single-decker, although certainly common throughout London, was more widespread in the shire counties and other metropolitan areas. This one is depicted on the longer-distance Green Line service from Dorking to London and was recorded on 20 July 1976. *Ian Whitmarsh*

Below: The unmistakable backdrop of Hyde Park Corner and one of the numerous London sightseeing vehicles in October 1977. Ever popular, the vehicles come with a guide and speaker system and are constantly patronised by visitors, especially those from overseas, despite the weather risk upstairs. *Ian Whitmarsh*

*Right:* Just in case things go wrong: a converted Leyland Freighter, freshly painted at Chiswick Works in the summer of 1963. *Tony Molyneaux*

*Above:* A little indulgence is asked for now on the part of the reader — who could resist this delightful time capsule view of the former Harrow pub at Studley Green near Stokenchurch. Along with several other pubs in the area, The Harrow was a regular stopping place for long-distance coach travel to and from London and the North. *Author's collection*

*Right:* In today's sense, it would be considered 'green' but I think red is more appropriate. One of the tourist horse buses on the outer circle at Regent's Park on 15 September 1979. *Ian Whitmarsh*

*Above:* Genuine horse-drawn transport in May 1964 and recorded at Hayes End. The temptation is to use the title of a contemporary television comedy series and that is indeed how Ian referred to the picture in his notes: Steptoe. *Ian Whitmarsh*

*Above right:* Another tourist attraction in the form of an organ grinder, unfortunately unnamed. Similarly unfortunate is the lack of information as to his exact location but his superb uniform of full morning dress is ample compensation. *Ian Whitmarsh*

*Right:* How many will state, 'I remember them', or 'I hired one like that once...' At a time when Morris Commercials, Leyland Terriers and Mk 1 Ford Transit vans were the latest vehicles, this is the EMI road-going fleet depicted at Southall in April 1977. *Ian Whitmarsh*

For many years there has been an engineering museum at the former Kew Bridge pumping station (and well worth a visit, too). Aside from the static attractions, there are also a number of other exhibits including visiting items. This was the scene in the yard in September 1977 with a restored 1933 Sentinel steam lorry partly uncovered for the benefit of the camera. *Ian Whitmarsh*

A slower form of transport: Brentford Dock on the Grand Union Canal. Brentford is the start of the canal proper and where it leaves the Thames for its 137-mile journey to Birmingham, incorporating no less than 166 locks. *Ian Whitmarsh*

*Above:* The entrance to the Thames at Brentford, overlooked by modern flats. The Grand Union Canal has also been featured in numerous films, one of the most renowned being the 1960s comedy The Bargee featuring Harry H. Corbett (of Steptoe & Son fame) and a very young Ronnie Barker as his bumbling but willing assistant. *Ian Whitmarsh*

*Right:* Another canal view, of St Pancras basin on the Regent's Canal. Just nine miles long, the Regent's Canal runs from the Thames at Limehouse to Paddington, where a connection is made with the arm of the Grand Junction Canal. Popular with walkers, the towpath affords a pleasant and quieter alternative to the nearby streets. *Ian Whitmarsh*

*Left:* Staying with the theme of transport, we now make a move underground. The stations on the Underground system we know today are very much an amalgamation of differing designs representing previous owners and construction at various periods in history. Shown here is Northfields, although the term 'Tube station' would be more accurate. In typical 1930s style, the  station displays an almost art-deco appearance which still appears modern 70 years later. *Ian Whitmarsh*

*Above:* The tube proper — well, the trains at least — and a view not necessarily seen by the travelling public. This is the line-up at the stops at Stanmore, most of the trains here probably destined for Bakerloo Line services. *Nick Britton*

*Left:* Uxbridge station in June 1977 and a special service with what was referred to as 'COP' stock. These units had been in service since the 1930s and were transferred to the District Line to replace the even older 'Q' stock. *Nick Britton*

*Right:* Uxbridge platform and a side view of the same train in June 1977. *Nick Britton*

*Below:* Against the buffer stops at Ealing Broadway at a quiet time of the afternoon, 7 October 1977. *Ian Whitmarsh*

*Left:* Baker Street station with a Metropolitan Line train. Aside from the variations in building style, notice the different forms of transport, with the Routemasters on the roadway above. *Nick Britton*

*Above:* Trailer car with the unusual number of 012345, recorded through the window at Stanmore. *Nick Britton*

PLATFORM 9

← WAY OUT →
CENTRAL LINE PLATFORMS 5 & 6
WESTERN REGION PLATFORMS 1, 2, 3 & 4

When there is no through District Line train,
passengers for stations beyond Earl's Court should
take the first train and change there.

EALING BROADWAY 8

*Left:* Ealing Broadway in October 1977 and a District Line train in the much-loved red livery. In the background is an aluminium coloured Central Line train. *Ian Whitmarsh*

*Above:* Variations in style at Ealing Broadway in June 1977. *Nick Britton*

*Above:* South of Ealing and a train of 'R' stock approaching journey's end at Wimbledon. Here is the interchange with what was then British Railways, the two systems sharing the same station but with the Tube lines on the north side. *Nick Britton*

*Right:* Typifying the clutter associated with the Tube system is this view of unit 3262 leaving the car sheds at Queen's Park. Despite the encouragement by both local and national governments for travellers to use public transport, this view shows one of the reasons why the existing system is difficult, if not impossible, to expand upon with little, if any, additional space available. *Ian Whitmarsh*

*Left:* Within the station at Queen's Park, unit 1075 pulls in ready for a departure with a train to Elephant & Castle on 25 July 1987. *Ian Whitmarsh*

*Above:* Train at the eastern terminus of the District Line at Upminster on 15 August 1987. This particular extension of the District Linemarked its fullest penetration eastwards, although further extensions west of London would come in later years. *Ian Whitmarsh*

The last surviving and operationally preserved electric locomotive from the Metropolitan Railway: No 12 *Sarah Siddons*, named after the 19th-century English actress. A second engine from the 20-strong class, No 5 John Hampden, is on display in the Covent Garden museum. *Nick Britton*

An unusual view of a Tube car from the Waterloo & City Line, also referred to as 'The Drain'. Photography of these vehicles is difficult to accomplish and thus rare, this particular vehicle being recorded at the mainline Waterloo station on an enthusiasts' day in the 1980s. *Nick Britton*

*Left:* The rarely photographed Post Office Railway that has been operational since 1927/8. The system is fully automated and carries mail beneath the London streets from Paddington in the west to the Whitechapel Delivery Office, also known as the Eastern Delivery Office. *Ian Whitmarsh*

*Above:* This is the control room at Mount Pleasant, the driverless trains being computer controlled and reaching speeds of 35mph between stations. A voltage drop allowed services to slow to a walking pace at any of the seven intermediate stations. Taken out of use in May 2003, the long-term future of the system is now in some doubt. *Ian Whitmarsh*

*Left:* From the lofty height of the Shell Building on the South Bank, a panoramic view of Waterloo station in 1964 and looking southwest towards Lambeth. The railway scene altered considerably in the 1980s with the building of Waterloo International although this expansion will also be short-lived, as 'Eurostar' trains will eventually use St Pancras. *Chris Webb*

*Above:* Last days of steam at Waterloo in May 1967 with 'West Country' class No 34024, formerly named *Tamar Valley*, leaving with empty stock. In the background is the Shell Building. Steam locomotives ceased operations from Waterloo in July 1967, the last of the London termini to witness regular steam workings. *David Barker*

*Left:* Two years earlier and steam in the suburbs. This is the area of Harrow-on-the-Hill on 16 August 1965. 'Black Five' No 45392 accelerates away from the station with the 8.15am through service from Nottingham to Marylebone. *David Barker*

*Above:* It was rare to see steam operation on the line north from Euston in the mid-1960s. However, BR Standard No 78056 hauls a 'dead' electric locomotive past Northwick Park and possibly bound for repair at Crewe. No E3025 was one of the first of the new electric engines introduced in connection with the modernisation of the West Coast main line, the overhead catenary for which can be seen in the background. *David Barker*

A somewhat grimy 'Britannia' class Pacific, No 70046 *Anzac*, leaving Harrow-on-the-Hill northbound with the 4.38pm Marylebone–Nottingham Victoria on 27 September 1965. This service used the former Great Central Railway through Brackley which was eventually closed as a through route soon after. *David Barker*

*Above:* While steam was being abandoned by British Railways, London Transport maintained a small fleet of ex-Great Western pannier tanks, which were purchased from British Railways and based at Neasden. They were used as maintenance trains. No L94 of the series was recorded at Harrow-on-the-Hill with a Moor Park–Neasden working on Christmas Eve 1965. *David Barker*

*Right:* Three years later, on 16 August 1968, L92 was photographed approaching Wembley Park on the same working. Around this time, a letter was published in The Times from a resident of the area who was disturbed to be awoken by what he perceived to be a 'steam engine whistle', confident in the knowledge that all such 'Kettles' had been abolished years before. Steam working by London Transport eventually ceased in 1971. *David Barker*

*Above:* Situated just off the GWR main line, Acton 'B' power station was another user of steam engines for shunting at a time when coal was being used as fuel for the electricity generation. Seen here is a small 0-4-0ST *Birkenhead* shunting on 21 March 1970. Built by Robert Stephenson & Hawthorn, the engine would eventually survive into preservation. *David Barker*

*Right:* Included because of the view of the M1 motorway under construction at Mill Hill in September 1966, preserved Gresley Pacific *Flying Scotsman* runs south past a scene of work with a special Gainsborough–Farnborough railtour. *David Barker*

*Above:* The modern railway — well in 1968, at least. A 'Western' class diesel passing Old Oak Common on the way west from Paddington in April 1968. *David Barker*

*Right:* The modern railway at Liverpool Street in April 1969. Diesel locomotives have replaced steam and office blocks dominate the skyline. Even so, the old style of platform canopy is still a reminder of times past, later to be swept away in the massive building programme at the station. *David Barker*

*Above:* Rail's future hope and competition against the road vehicle —
Willesden Freightliner depot in October 1967. *David Barker*

*Right:* Contrasting forms of transport at Willesden in March 1970 with the
Grand Junction Canal passing underneath the railway. Neglected for many years,
the waterway has enjoyed a renaissance in recent times with a new interchange as well
as encouragement to use the canal for general freight haulage. *David Barker*

*Above:* Line-up at King's Cross suburban station on 30 August 1968, typifying the uniform if necessarily bland image of the railways of the time. Alongside is St Pancras station. *David Barker*

*Right:* A similar image at Waterloo although electric traction was the norm. Units 5906, 5905 and 5502 are seen on 21 May 1988. *Ian Whitmarsh*

Having enjoyed views of land and water transport, we conclude with air travel, albeit on terra firma. London Heathrow in 1966 with a Vickers VC10 waiting on the tarmac. *Chris Webb*